Live • Work • Play • Learn

GALLOPADE INTERNATIONAL

Gallopade International is introducing SAT words that kids need to know in our books. The SAT words in this book have a gray box around them. Students can look up the definitions and increase their vocabulary. Happy Learning!

Gallopade is proud to be a member and supporter of these educational organizations and associations:

Association for the Study of African American Life and History
National Alliance of Black School Educators
American Booksellers Association
American Library Association
International Reading Association
National Association for Gifted Children
The National School Supply and Equipment Association
The National Council for the Social Studies
Museum Store Association
Association of Partners for Public Lands
Association of Booksellers for Children

At the time of publication, all websites referenced in this document were valid. However, due to the changing nature of the Internet, some addresses may change or the content become less relevant.

It's Your World Books

Africa: A Safari Through Its Amazing Nations!

Australia: The Land Down Under for Mates of All Ages!

Canada: The Maple Leaf Melting Pot Country!

China: A Great Wall Runs Thru It!

Egypt: An Ancient Land of Lore; a Modern Land of Oil and More!

France: The Ooh-La-La Country Everyone Loves!

Germany: The Country of Fairytale Castles and Cutting Edge Science!

Greece: A Volcanic Land of Ancient Olympic Origins!

India: Land of Six Senses and Intriguing Mystery!

Italy: The Country of Amazing Fountains and Awesome Arts!

Japan: An Island Country of Endless Intrigue!

Mexico: A Colorful Land of Exotic Culture!

Middle East: Ancient Countries of Current Events Headlines!

Russia: The Great Bear and Its Dramatic History!

South America: A Continent of Countries of Amazing Proportions!

United Kingdom: The Country of Ships, Sealing Wax, Cabbages, and Kings!

Other Carole Marsh Related Titles:

The Mystery of the Ancient Acropolis

Greek for Kids

Table of Contents

A Letter from the Author

From the desk of
CAROLE MARSH

Hey kids,

It's your world! It really, really is!
Of course, you already know that, don't you?
You surf the 'net, listen to satellite radio, watch television shows and movies set all around the globe—kids today are much more "worldly" than in the past, and that's a good thing!

Now's a great time to learn something about another country—such as Greece. Why? Because one day, you might actually visit there (if you have not already!). You might go to school there—many colleges have ties with international schools around the globe. You might even go on to work in a foreign country!

Many companies have positions in other countries. Companies are "going global" as fast as they can. They have branch offices, manufacturing plants, and customer service centers scattered around the globe!

So, ready or not: YOU are a Citizen of the World! And you'll want to be a good one.
How do you do that? You'll find out everything you can about that country, how it's the same, and how it's different from your own country. What language is spoken there? What customs do the people observe? What foods do they enjoy? What do they do for fun? What has happened in this part of the world and what is happening there now? It's fun ... and the more you learn, the more you will enjoy whatever global opportunity comes your way!

This book is a good place to start your learning journey—so take advantage of the world— IT'S YOUR WORLD, after all ... and guess what? It's a BIG world, after all!

Happy traveling and learning,

Carole Marsh
Always with passport in hand!

Why Should We Care About Greece?

Greece is one of the most intriguing countries in the world. This beautiful country and its rich history make it a desirable destination for travelers from all over the world. Everyone wants to see the Acropolis, the ancient Parthenon, the National Archaeological Museum, the beautiful islands of Mykonos, Hydra and Santorini, the Mediterranean Ocean, the olive growing region of Kalamata, and so much more!

Greek culture combines a slower-paced lifestyle with a strong work ethic. Greece has some of the most gorgeous beaches in the world, and with its warm Mediterranean climate, you can spend a lot of time enjoying them! And Greek food is some of the tastiest and healthiest cuisine anywhere!

One day, you might visit Greece to see the location of the original Olympic Games, sail on a boat to Crete, study philosophy at the University of Athens, get a job as a fisherman, or work as an archaeologist. It could happen!

Write home about it!
What will your postcard from Greece say?

Top Fast Greece Facts!

Important facts to remember about the country of Greece:

- Greece is officially known as Elliniki Dimokratia, the Hellenic Republic.
- Greece has a President and a Prime Minister.
- Greece is governed by the Constitution of Greece.
- Greece is one of the 50 founding members of the United Nations and is also a member of the European Union. It is a strategic ally of the United States.
- Greece has more than 16 million visitors every year. During the Olympic Games in 2004, over 18 million people visited!
- The capital of Greece is Athens.
- The official language is Greek.
- The currency used is the euro (and the drachma).
- The Greek national anthem is "Hymn to Freedom."
- Their national motto is "Freedom or Death."

Now, you figure out the rest!

1. This is the Greek ___ ___ ___ ___ .

2. The ___ ___ ___ ___ ___ ___ ___ ___ ___ ___ of Greece is about 11 million people.

3. This is the national ___ ___ ___ ___ ___ ___ of Greece. ⟶

4. The Hellenic Republic is the ___ ___ ___ ___ ___ ___ ___ ___ name of Greece.

5. Greece had more than 18 ___ ___ ___ ___ ___ ___ ___ visitors in 2004.

6. ___ ___ ___ ___ ___ ___ is named for the Greek goddess Athena.

Where in the World Is Greece?

- Greece is located in southern Europe. It is a country with more than 400 islands!
- Greece has several neighbors, including Albania, Macedonia, Bulgaria, and Turkey.
- Greek Independence Day is March 25.
- Greece is surrounded on three sides by four bodies of water—the Ionian Sea, the Mediterranean Sea, the Aegean Sea, and the Sea of Crete.
- Greece is the original home of the ancient Olympic Games.
- The highest point in Greece is Mount Olympus (2,917 meters above sea level).
- The Parthenon, which was built as a temple for the Greek goddess Athena, is located on the Acropolis, a hill that overlooks Athens.
- Some of the best olives and virgin olive oils in the world are produced in Kalamata, the second largest city in Greece.
- Piraeus is the second largest harbor in the Mediterranean Sea, after Marseilles in France.

Do You Know?

1. What percentage of Greece is mountainous?
   a. 30   b. 90   c. 80   d. 100

2. In Greek mythology, Mount Olympus was known as the "home of the gods."
   Zeus was king of the: a. Greeks   b. sea   c. gods

   Aphrodite was the goddess of: a. the sun   b. water   c. love

Athletes and Philosophers!
Scientists and Architects!

Western civilization was born about 2,500 years ago in ancient Greece! Achievements of the ancient Greeks in government, science, philosophy, the arts, architecture, and sports still influence our lives today! Ancient Greece was made up of many independent *polis*, or city-states. Each city-state consisted of a town and its surrounding villages and farmland. The first democratic governments were introduced in the more advanced Greek city-states. The most advanced of those were Athens and Sparta.

Greek city-states were not united as one nation, but they had the same language, religion, and culture. Greek life was dominated by religion. As a result, they built the largest, most beautiful temples as a tribute to their gods and goddesses. Some of them, including the Parthenon, still stand today! Ancient Greeks were proud of their way of life and prized their freedom, stressing individualism and the value of creative thinking.

Crosswords!
Use your new knowledge to fill in the crossword puzzle.

Across

1. Western civilization was born in _____ Greece.
3. *Polis* is the Greek term for _____.
5. _____ was an advanced city-state in ancient Greece.

Down

2. _____ is an ancient temple.
4. Ancient Greeks prized their _____.
6. The first _____ governments were introduced in Greece.

The Amazing History of Greece!

Greece has an exciting history which helped shape the culture of the world we live in today! Our language, architecture, art, and even our schools were all influenced by the people of ancient Greece. During the Greek Classical Period (500 – 336 B.C.E.), the people of Athens created a democratic system of government, similar to what we have today. The amazing Parthenon on the Acropolis was built without the modern tools we have today. Sophocles and Euripides wrote great tragedies, which we still read and perform today!

Alexander the Great

By the end of the Classical Period, Greek military commander Alexander the Great had conquered most of the ancient world. Countries including Syria, Gaza, and Egypt became part of the Greek empire. This began the Hellenistic Period, (336 – 146 B.C.E.), which is considered Greece's greatest era! Greek politics, law, religion, and literature were introduced to the rest of the world.

After the Nazi occupation of Greece in World War II (1941 – 1944), a struggle for control of the country led to a Civil War that began in 1946. The war lasted until 1949 when the Communist Party was defeated.

Today, Greece is an independent and beautiful country. Even though it struggles with unemployment and other modern issues, the people of Greece are confident their future will be a bright one!

Timeline!

Number these events in the order that they took place, first to last.

___ End of the Greek Civil War

___ Recent Olympic Games in Athens

___ Classical Period

___ Hellenistic Period

___ Beginning of the Greek Civil War

___ Nazi occupation of Greece

Great Greeks!

Matching!

Match these famous Greek folks with their accomplishments.

A. Plato

B. Sophocles

C. Homer

D. Thespis

E. Alexander the Great

F. Hippocrates

1. ____ I am considered one of the greatest military leaders in history and was never defeated in battle. I became king of Macedonia after the death of my father, Philip II.

2. ____ I was a classical Greek philosopher and mathematician. As a student of the great philosopher Socrates, I carried on his work after his death. I wrote one of the most influential works in the history of Western philosophy called *The Republic*.

3. ____ A legendary poet, the ancient Greeks thought of me as a historical figure; however modern scholars believe my works were written by many poets over time. I am credited with writing the *Iliad* and the *Odyssey*.

4. ____ I was a playwright. I have been acknowledged for influencing the development of drama and improving the development of characters in plays. Two of my most famous works are *Oedipus the King* and *Antigone*, which are known as "tragedies," a form of theatre art.

5. ____ A physician, I am considered one of the most influential figures in the history of medicine and am called "the father of medicine." As the founder of the Hippocratic school of medicine, I was the first to believe that illness was not punishment from the gods.

6. ____ I am believed to be the first person to ever perform on stage as an actor in a play. Many believe that I invented acting and to this day actors are referred to as thespians, in my honor.

Guts and Glory Greek Style!

A. Many thousands of people died when it hit the city-state of Athens during the second year of the Peloponnesian War in 430 B.C.E. A victory for the Athenian army appeared possible until this arrived and some historians believe it was the reason the war was lost.

_____

B. It is considered one of the largest in 10,000 years of geological history. Its occurrence in 1625 B.C.E. is believed to have caused the end of the Minoan civilization on the island of Crete.

_____

C. He was the leader of a secret organization that sought Greek independence from the Ottoman Empire. His invasion of Moldavia in 1821 was the beginning of the Greek War of Independence.

_____

D. They did not believe in the luxuries of life, leisure time, or fancy foods. Simplicity, self-discipline, and self-denial were consistent throughout their society. The lives of its citizens were designed to serve the state until age sixty.

_____

E. It is one of the most important events in Greek mythology and it is said to have originated after Paris stole Helen from her husband Menelaus. It is depicted in many works of Greek literature and art. A horse is a central character in the story!

_____

Mixed Up!
Match the paragraph to the word that the paragraph describes.

SPARTANS

____

ALEXANDER YPSILANTI

____

BLACK PLAGUE

____

VOLCANIC ERUPTION OF SANTORINI

____

TROJAN WAR

____

Hammer and Point!

Remember how it feels to have someone take your picture? You have to stand still forever! Imagine how long models had to pose for the great Greek sculptors! To create their art, Greek sculptors mostly used bronze and marble. They are both very difficult to work with.

The artists used a technique called "hammer and point" to carve the magnificent statues of ancient Greece. They held the point, or a chisel, against the marble and hit it as hard as possible with the hammer again and again, breaking the stone. A variety of points were used until the sculpture was complete. That's hard work!

The Classical period of Ancient Greece produced some of the most beautiful sculptures the world has ever seen. Polykleitos, born in 450 B.C.E., has been called the creator of the Classical Period. He created sculptures showing natural human poses and balance. As the art of sculpture progressed, Lysippos made the heads of his figures smaller and the body longer. This technique made his sculptures look more like a real human body!

Discus Thrower

Many of the sculptures created during the Classical and Hellenistic periods of ancient Greece still exist today! The Discus Thrower (Discobolos) is one of the most famous marble pieces in history. A copy of it can be seen at the National Museum of Rome, Italy.

Draw your own sculpture!
Get out your pencil or crayons and draw a sculpture of one of your favorite people!

Mystery Homer!

Homer

Do you like poetry? Poetry was very important in ancient Greece.

Homer was a legendary Greek poet. The Greeks believe he existed, but there are many versions of when and if he lived. Historians have no reliable information on where he was born, how long he lived, or the exact time period. That makes his life somewhat of a mystery! It is believed that he was the author of the epic poems the *Iliad* and the *Odyssey*, which are both based on the great Trojan War.

The *Iliad* tells the story of Achilles, an invincible warrior with one weak spot—one of his heels. The *Odyssey* follows the travels of Odysseus, the king of Ithaca. He helped devise a scheme to drag a hollow Trojan horse into an enemy's city with soldiers hidden inside.

The Trojan War

Many believe that Homer did not actually exist in Greek history but was a fictitious name used to identify many of the poems that were passed on from the Mycenaean civilization. This was the time period during which the Trojan War was believed to have been fought. The Trojan War is an important part of what helped to define Greek culture over time.

Word Play!

Homer created his poetry for all to use and enjoy. Use the letters from the *Odyssey* to make as many words with three letters or more as you can.

THE ODYSSEY

_____   _____

_____   _____

_____   _____

_____   _____

_____   _____

_____   _____

_____   _____

The Parthenon, A Site to See!

The Acropolis towers high above the city of Athens. It is one of the most famous landmarks in Europe! The classical Greek architecture has become a symbol of the city. Built around 2,500 years ago, the Acropolis has several temples. The most important is the Parthenon, dedicated to Athena, a Greek goddess. Its massive foundations were made of limestone, and the columns were made of marble. The temple's main function was to shelter a statue of Athena made of gold and ivory.

The Parthenon has functioned most importantly as a Greek temple, but has also been a treasury, a fortress, a church, and a mosque.

There are no absolute straight lines on the Parthenon!

The temple was opened to the public the moment it was finished.

Approximately 13,000 stones were used to build the Parthenon.

The Parthenon is a large temple, but it is by no means the largest one in Greece.

Create your very own travel pamphlet.
Concentrate on an area that interests you. Perhaps you enjoyed learning about the people. Or maybe it was the monuments that interested you. Fold a piece of paper into three sections. This will give you six areas on which to put information.

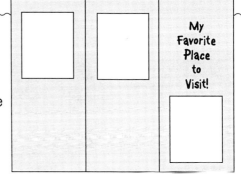

My Favorite Place to Visit!

Spit on It!

Customs and culture vary widely from country to country. Sometimes they vary in different regions of the same country. Here are customs and cultural differences observed by the Greek people!

- The handshake is a common greeting.
- It is polite to arrive late for a dinner or party!
- The fork is held in the left hand and the knife in the right. You hold them the opposite way!
- Moving your head downward means "yes." Moving your head upward means "no."
- Children are often named after saints, and they celebrate their saint's "name day" or "feast day" as well as their own birthday!
- Spitting is thought to ward off evil and prevent misfortune! Fishermen might spit on their nets to ensure a good catch, or a student might spit on a paper to avoid a bad grade.
- Most people in Greece don't begin eating dinner until 9 p.m., and the meal may last for hours!
- Football is the favorite sport of Greece. You call it soccer!

Create your own!
Customs and cultural activities can help define who we are. Think about your family and friends and come up with some new customs for everyone to try.

A lump of sugar in the glove of the bride is thought to make for a sweet marriage.

It's All Greek to Me!

The official language in Greece is Greek. They use a different alphabet. They use their very own Greek alphabet.

Match it up!

Below are some common Greek phrases or words. See if you can match them to the English word.

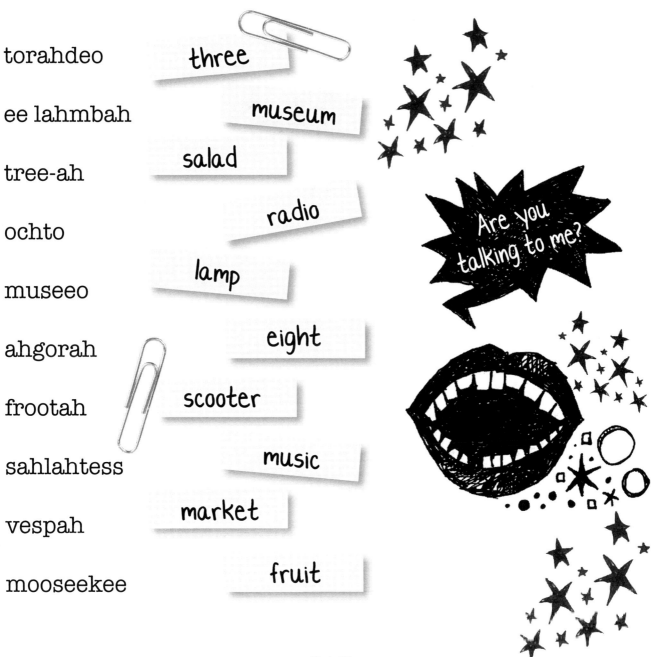

torahdeo

ee lahmbah

tree-ah

ochto

museeo

ahgorah

frootah

sahlahtess

vespah

mooseekee

three

museum

salad

radio

lamp

eight

scooter

music

market

fruit

Are you talking to me?

Happy Holidays!

Greece celebrates many holidays and festivals. Many of these holidays are religious, including **Easter** and **Christmas**. Christian Greeks also celebrate **Saint Basil's Day** on January 1st. Many Greeks will give each other gifts on this day rather than on Christmas.

Greece holds many festivals throughout the year. Most cities have a patron saint, and once a year they celebrate their saint's feast day. They attend church and then have a party.

Other holidays include **Independence Day** on March 25th and **Ochi Day** on October 28th. Ochi Day is the day that Greece entered World War II on the side of the Allies. On that day, the Greek prime minister said "no" ("ochi") to an Italian invasion.

Write it down!

Pretend you are visiting Greece. Write a letter to your best friend. Tell him or her about a Greek festival. Be sure to describe the party and what kind of food you ate.

PRESENT

Greece on the Stage and in the Museums!

ADMIT ONE 151332

The art and music culture of ancient Greece has had an enormous impact on modern times. Greek mythology, tragedy, and comedy have influenced the literature of other countries.

2.

3.

Notes

1. The *syrto* is one of the most popular forms of Greek folk dance.

2. Most ancient Greek buildings have crumbled with time. This relief from the Parthenon demonstrates how grand the art really was.

3. *Winged Nike of Samothrace* is the most famous statue of the Hellenistic period.

4. The muses of comedy and tragedy from ancient Greece continue to represent theater today.

5. Hercules was one of the greatest heroes in Greek mythology. He is famous for his strength.

GO!

1.

5.

ADMIT ONE 151332

4.

What's for Dinner?

The Greek diet is a very healthy diet. Known as the Mediterranean diet, it includes olive oil, salads, lamb, and vegetables. Take a look below and see the kinds of foods you could expect to eat if you visited Greece.

Spanakopita is a small pie filled with feta cheese and spinach.

A popular main dish is **moussaka.** It is made with meat and baked eggplant.

Baklava is a dessert made with nuts, honey, and pastry.

Souvlaki is grilled meat and vegetables served with pita bread.

RECIPE

Always ask an adult for help when cooking!

Greek Salad

INGREDIENTS

2 cups sliced tomatoes
2 1/2 cups cucumbers, peeled & quartered
1/2 cup diced red pepper
1/2 cup diced green pepper
1/4 cup diced sweet red onion

1/4 cup pitted black kalamata olives
1/4 cup shredded fresh garden basil leaves
1/4 cup balsamic vinaigrette dressing
1/2 cup crumbled feta cheese

mmmmmm...this was good!

DIRECTIONS

• Mix the tomatoes, cucumbers, red pepper, green pepper, onion, olives, and basil in a large salad bowl.
• Coat evenly with balsamic vinaigrette dressing by tossing with salad tongs.
• Crumble the feta cheese on top and serve. Refrigerate leftovers.

Makes 6 to 8 servings

Many Greek foods were influenced by the Turks!

And the Gold Medal Goes to...GREECE!

Actually, all the medals did back then! The first Olympic Games on record began in 776 B.C.E. in Olympia, Greece. The ancient Greeks had a love for competition and sporting competition was at the top of the list. The Olympic Games were a series of athletic events for participants from many of the city-states throughout Greece.

The Olympic events were held at the Sanctuary of Zeus at Olympia. Each competitor spoke Greek, shared the same religious beliefs, and came from as far away as the Black Sea in Turkey. Unlike today, only 23 events were contested in the ancient games! The Olympics were divided into three categories—men's track and field events, equestrian events, and boys' events. The very first event to be contested was the "stadion," a race 600 feet in length.

After the ancient games ended, it took 1,503 years for the Olympics to return. The first modern Olympics were held in Athens, Greece, in 1896. The man who was responsible for championing their return in 1894 was a Frenchman named Baron Pierre de Coubertin. His plan was to host them in his native Paris in 1900. However, representatives from 34 countries were so excited by the idea that they convinced him to move the games up to 1896 and have Athens act as the host!

**Jesse Owens, USA
Olympic Athlete**

Be a Coloring Champion!

Get out your crayons. Draw a picture of the athletes running the first Olympic foot race!

The Birthplace of Democracy!

Athena is the Greek goddess of wisdom, war, the arts, industry, justice, and skill. She is also the namesake of Greece's capital city, Athens! The history of Athens and its people dates back 4,500 years. That makes it one of the oldest cities in the world!

In 1400 B.C.E., Athens was controlled by the Mycenaean civilization, which is named after another Greek city, Mycenae. Archaeologists have discovered that the Mycenaean people were great engineers and built outstanding palaces, bridges, and tombs. They were also very wealthy!

By the 9th century, Athens had once again regained its power. Today, Athens is a vibrant city with many museums, world class hotels, cuisine, and of course, historical places! In the center of Athens is the Theatre of Dionysos. It was built in 600 B.C.E. and seated close to 20,000 people. That's a lot of people in one place!

At the Parliament building in Syntagma Square, you can watch the changing of the guard, which happens once an hour!

Acropolis of Athens

Word Fun!

List the historical landmarks and other attractions in Athens.

Athens has given the world three of mankind's greatest philosophers: Socrates, Plato, and Aristotle.

Historical Landmarks	Attractions

Greece Did It First!

Word Fun!

This is fun to do with someone else. Ask a friend for words to substitute for the blanks in the story. Their word substitutions will have a humorous effect when the resulting story is then read aloud.

It's Warm in Here!
The first person to harness the power of steam was the Greek scientist Heron.

Will it Sink?
Archimedes first discovered the principle that tells us if an object will float in water.

Let's Find Out Who Is Stronger!
According to historical records, the first Olympic Games were held in Olympia in 776 B.C.E.

I want to be the first person to _____
(ACTION VERB)

across _____! I've been training for this
(COUNTRY)

since _____. I'm in_____ shape.
(MONTH)   (ADJECTIVE)

My _____ adventure will begin on
(ADJECTIVE)

_____. I won't be hard to miss.
(FAVORITE HOLIDAY)

I'll be the one wearing a _____
(COLOR)

_____ and a pair of matching
(ARTICLE OF CLOTHING)

_____. My faithful friends
(FOOTWEAR)

_____ and
(FAMOUS ATHLETE)

_____ will be there to cheer for me.
(CARTOON CHARACTER)

I'm bringing my _____ along for good luck.
(NOUN)

I'm confident I'll be the first!

Put On Your Sun Block!
Aristarchus, a Greek astronomer, was the first person to suggest that the sun, not the moon, was at the center of the universe.

I Have a Question, Dad!
Greek historian Herodotus is considered the father of history.

O-live You!
The first cultivation of the olive tree took place in Greece.

Greek Mythology

Myths are stories that use magic and symbols to explain events and people. The stories aren't always true, but people believe them to be true! Greek Mythology explains the great heroes, rituals, and gods of the ancient Greeks. Below are some of the gods that star in Greek Mythology.

Zeus, who is known as the ruler of Mount Olympus and king of the gods, ruled the sky and thunder. To represent his power, he was given the mythological symbols of an eagle and thunderbolt.

Aphrodite, the Greek goddess of love and beauty, was said to cause any man who even looked at her to fall in love!

Zeus

Apollo, son of Zeus and one of the most complex characters in Greek mythology, was god of the sun, poetry, and music. Apollo was also worshiped in the ancient Roman religion.

Greek mythology is exciting to read about and study!

Apollo

Word Fun!
Pretend you have met a Greek god or goddess. Write five questions that you would ask him or her.

Example: Where were you born?

1. _____?

2. _____?

3. _____?

4. _____?

5. _____?

Beware of Trojan Horses!

What would you think if someone gave you a rocking horse large enough to fit 30 men inside? You might be a little suspicious, just as the Trojans should have been when General Odysseus and his army left a huge wooden horse outside the gates of their city!

According to Greek mythology, the goddesses Athena, Aphrodite, and Hera quarreled. King Zeus sent each of them to Paris of Troy to decide who was the "fairest" of the three! Paris named Aphrodite the fairest. As a thank you, she made Helen of Troy fall in love with Paris.

Helen's husband, Menelaus, was very angry and led his warriors to attack the city of Troy. For 10 years, the warriors tried to invade the city, but it was protected by strong, high walls that were hard to break down. Finally, the Greek general Odysseus suggested they leave a "gift" for Troy that would announce the end of the war.

Helen of Troy

The gift was a wooden horse which was hollowed out so that 30 men could hide inside! When the Trojans saw the horse, they believed they had won the war. After they pulled it through the gates and fell asleep, the troops inside climbed out, opened the gates, and the Greek army overtook Troy!

Revealing Answer!

Unscramble the letters to reveal the "fairest" goddess.

Cross off the first two letters
Cross off the letter W
Cross off the seventh letter
Cross off the fourth letter from the end
Cross off the sixteenth letter
Cross off the fifteenth letter

G O P A T I X H W O R D Y E N Z

The Greek War of Independence

Did you know that Greece was not always a free nation? The Turkish Ottoman army first crossed into Europe in 1354 and began to build an empire that would rule many countries for centuries. Having defeated Bulgaria and then Serbia, the Ottomans moved south and overtook the city of Athens in 1458. This would begin almost 400 years of Ottoman occupation in Greece.

The proud Greek citizens fought heroically against the occupation and were able to hold out in the Peloponnese peninsula in southern Greece until 1460. By 1500, the Ottoman Empire had taken over the majority of Greece. However, the mountain areas were left untouched and provided a safe hiding place for many Greeks who wanted to be free. Others migrated to Western Europe.

In 1814, a secret society called the "friendly society" began the long process of planning a rebellion. With assistance from wealthy Greeks in other countries, Alexander Ypsilanti led an invasion of Moldavia in 1821, which was the start of the eight-year war for independence.

The war ended in 1829. King Otto was named the first modern King of Greece in 1832, making Greece an independent, sovereign power.

King Otto

Cross it off!

Starting with the first letter, cross off every other letter to reveal where King Otto was born.

XSQAPLPZXBDUKROGF

_____

FATUISMTZRLIHAP

_____

Pick an Island, Any Island!

The Greek Islands have been described as some of the most beautiful in the world! The Greek Islands are grouped into several clusters, including the Saronic islands, Dodecanese islands, and Aegean islands. Amazingly, the Greek islands are located on three different seas, the Mediterranean, Aegean, and Ionian!

The Islands of Greece

The Isle of Crete is the largest Greek island and fifth largest in the entire Mediterranean. One of the most popular vacation destinations for Europeans, Crete offers a long coastline, sandy beaches, and the warm, blue waters of the Mediterranean. Crete also has a rich ancient history as the home of the Minoan civilization. Archaeologists have found ruins on Crete dating back to 1700 B.C.E.

Artemis

The island of Mykonos has been described in Greek mythology as the location where Poseidon and Hercules destroyed giants that opposed Zeus. Mykonos is now one of the most popular tourist destinations in Greece. Delos, an island located opposite Mykonos, is known as one the greatest archaeological sites in the world and the birthplace of the gods Apollo and Artemis.

Did you know that there are over 6,000 islands and islets that belong to Greece? Only 220 are inhabited by people and 70 of those have less than 100 residents!

Figure it out!

List three islands on each of the following seas:

Mediterranean	Aegean	Ionian
_____	_____	_____
_____	_____	_____
_____	_____	_____

Fashion Statements of the Gods! Ancient Greek Fashion

What color was ancient Greek clothing? If you said "white," you are wrong! Greek clothing was usually homemade, dyed different colors, and decorated with beautiful designs. Ancient Greek clothing was designed to be loose fitting and functional. Most Greek clothing was made from wool or linen.

The tunic was worn by both men and women. The length of the garment depended upon whether it was for a man or woman and the job that person performed. The *chiton*, a type of tunic usually worn by men, was made of light linen or silk which was good for working outside, especially during the hot Greek summers. The *peplos* was a full length women's tunic made from heavier wool. It could be worn in different ways.

The ancient Greeks preferred not to wear shoes, especially indoors. When they did, leather sandals or boots were the choice of footwear.

peplos

Dress up!

Help Christina get dressed for her tour of Greece! Choose which outfit she'll wear. Color the clothing, and draw a line from the piece of clothing to Christina or cut the clothing out and dress her up!

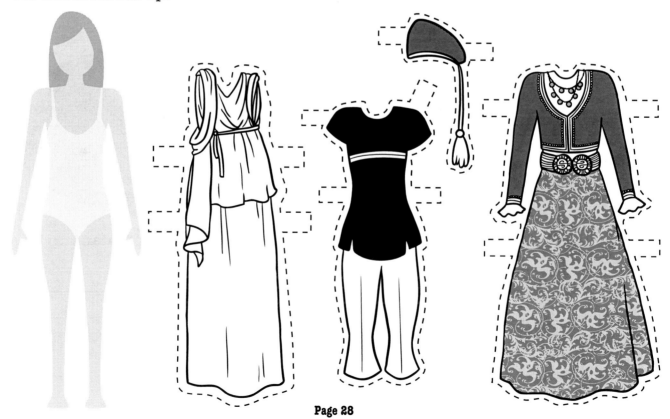

Assorted Architecture!

Figure it out!

Use the following clues to figure out this famous structure in Athens, Greece.

- There are three separate buildings atop this one famous structure.
- The most well known of the three began construction in 447 B.C.E. and was a temple for Athena.
- At its top is a building that was used as an entryway and façade for the building above.
- The third building is a temple on the north side of this structure and derived its name from the Greek hero Erichthonius.
- It sits high above Athens and was therefore easy to defend in ancient times.
- Its name means "the citadel or high fortified area of an ancient Greek city."

It's All Greek to Me!

The alphabet used in Greece is different than the English alphabet, although the word alphabet originated from the Greek language! There are many Greek words you use often. Here are a few!

English Word	Original Greek Word
academy	akadimia
bacteria	bactirio
category	catigoria
diploma	diploma
encyclopedia	encyclopaidia
gymnastics	gymnastiki
hero	iroas
mathematics	mathimatica
ocean	oceanos
paradise	paradeisos
scholastic	scholastikos
theater	theatro
union	enosi
vandalism	vandalismos
zoology	zoologia

Further Resources

US Embassy in Greece
91 Vasilisis Sophias Avenue
10160 Athens, Greece
Phone: 30-210-721-2951
AthensAmEmb@state.gov

United Nations
2 United Nations Plaza
New York, NY 10017

Greek National Tourism Organization at Athens
26A, Amalias Avenue
Phone: 30-210-331-0392

Hellenic Tourism Organization
Olympic Tower, 645 Fifth Avenue, Suite 903
New York, NY 10022
Phone: (212) 421-5777
Fax: (212) 826-6940
http://www.greektourism.com
info@greektourism.com

Interesting Websites

http://www.ancient-greece.org/

http://www.newacropolismuseum.gr/

http://www.greekmythology.com/

http://www.greekisland.co.uk/

http://www.aegeansea.com/

Answer Key

Page 7
1. flag 2. population 3. symbol 4. official
5. million 6. Athens

Page 8
1. C 2. Zeus-c, Aphrodite-c

Page 9

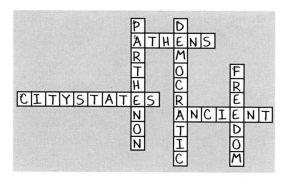

Page 10
5, 6, 1, 2, 4, 3

Page 11
1. E 2. A 3. C 4. B 5. F 6. D

Page 12
Spartans – D, Alexander Ypsilanti – C,
Black Plague – A, Volcanic Eruption of
Santorini – B, Trojan War - E

Page 17
torahdeo - radio
ee lahmbah - lamp
treeah - three
ochto - eight
museeo - museum
ahgorah - market
frootah - fruit
sahlahtess - salad
vespah – scooter
mooseekee - music

Page 22
Landmarks
Parthenon, Acropolis, Theatre of Dionysos,
Syntagma Square
Attractions
museums, hotels, restaurants

Page 25
Aphrodite

Page 26
Salzburg, Austria

Page 27
Answers will vary

Page 29
Acropolis